This may sound a bit crass, but would you like to play with my ass?

My ass is big, my ass is strong,
when you play with my ass,
you're never wrong.

My ass is firm, my ass is wiggly, but if it eats too much, it can get jiggly.

My ass is the best at show,
every time I bring out my ass,
it gets a lot of dough.

Sometime you just need to give my ass a little kick. Don't worry; my ass is just extra thick.

This ass is tasty and sweet,
because of all the sugar it does eat.

This ass has pals that are friendly.
My ass is always running around
with my pussy.

My ass is mild. But feed it beans, and it becomes wild.

Ride my ass as hard as you can.
Prove it, and you'll be a real man.

My ass is washed and clean.
If it was dirty, playing with it
would be rather obscene.

Done with my ass? Move on to the next thing that will make you shocked. Would you like to play with my big, fat cock?

Dear friends,

Thank you very much for reading my book.
My name is Gary Galvin, and I'm a stay at home dad who wants to have some fun :).

Did you enjoy the book?
Did it make you giggle, or laugh?
If you like the book, please do me a huge favor and write me a review on Amazon.
I love you read your review. It means a lot to me and really encourages me to create more books for you.

Enjoy!

Gary Galvin

Have someone to share the fun with?

Get a physical copy of this book on Amazon and give it to them as a gag gift, and I promise they will remember it forever! (By doing so, you will also buy me a cup of coffee and I'll be very thankful :)

For more fun books like this, visit www.funbooksforyou.com.

Other book by Gary Galvin

Would you like to play with my Pussy?

Gary Galvin

Printed in Great Britain
by Amazon